# THE
# CAR
# MASUTRA ©

# THE CAR MASUTRA

## THE MAN WHO LOVES HIS CAR !!

THE ESSENTIAL GUIDE
TO
THE ULTIMATE ACT OF LOVE
BY

# MARY BIRD

LEFT AND LEFT AGAIN

Productions & Publications

A Left And Left Again book

First published in the United Kingdom by
Left And Left Again in 2006

Left And Left Again
37 High Street
Ixworth
Bury St Edmunds
Suffolk IP31 2HJ
United Kingdom
www.leftandleftagain.co.uk

British Library Cataloguing Data.

Bird, Mary
    The Car Masutra: The man who
    loves his car 1. Men. Cars. Humour.
    Self help. Interpersonal relationships
    with women.

ISBN 978-0-9552149-1-2

The Car Masutra ©
For the man who loves his car ©

www.carmasutra.com
www.forthemanwholoveshiscar.com

Typeset and printed by Ink In Print Ltd
Printed in Great Britain using paper from
sustainable forests

THE CAR MASUTRA  TM Pending

# CONTENTS

"If it's happiness you want, change yourself, not other people: It is easier to protect your feet with shoes, than to carpet the whole world."

Anon

For my three babies

...and for all the men who love their cars
...and the women who love their men!!

A special thank you to all the car lovers that
have allowed me to have a giggle at their
expense!!

Thank you guys, you know who you are!! XXX

And of course an even bigger thank you to my
girl friends and female associates who shared the
laughs with me, believed in it all and believed in me!!

Thank you, you know who you are too.

"Strange old world really, some jokes never change!!"

P.S. Neither do men!!

# WHERE IT ALL CAME FROM!!

JOHN 1 : 1-3

# THE BIG BANG

And what a bang it was !!! The biggest bang of all bangs and the one that produced an outcome of mind curdling proportions. Yet amongst this vastness of a universe was a planet whose name was earth, and upon it was placed…"Man" a cheery little fellow really, running around happy starkers in the garden without a credit card, Blackberry or personal trainer to his name.

But God decided that "Man" should NOT be alone. The end of the Gentleman's club was already in sight, the male domain of the public bar was beginning to shake and words like "equality" were forming in the shape of prosecution lawyers, as a mate was created for him.

However, God insisted that this mate was going to be a complementary being; He would have a companion, and a friend, a partner… his other half. A kindred spirit that would be the apple of his eye…his hearts desire…his fulfilment of manhood and everything his mother was to him!

Man agreed "it was good"

Although the actual first meeting between man and woman is not strictly recorded (no blind date or surprise surprise in those days) history has shown that man was rather expecting this new being to have been created more or less on the same lines as himself. Okay a few lumps and bumps in alternative places could be a rather interesting new angle, and prevent evolution growing the man with one big right arm, but what he faced was something much more complex, much more frightening yet much more gorgeously appealing than any thing his little eyes had ever befallen before.

Her name was "WOMAN".

Oh what a happy man he was... but how short was the party....

For man was totally unaware that God had a sense of humour.

It is now that I turn to that fateful day, where mans blissful ignorance was destroyed, where his heart was nailed to a mortgage, when the wage packet was never quite enough. The children began eating him out of house and home and the wife started talking about running her own business!

For as woman took the fruit from the tree of knowledge and ate, she became increasingly aware of her partners lack of assets.... except what dangled down swinging around, taking the air.
His attempt to understand the woman's source of amusement, lead to him taking of the fruit too, only to become overwhelmingly aware of the out come of listening to woman, and the devastating consequences that it held.

He had been created with the apparatus of his ego in his ultimate area of vulnerability!! Pride began to raise it's ugly head, and so did the dangly bit.

From then on every thing changed. Man had many a sleepless night working out how he was going to rectify this unfortunate situation he now found himself in. It was no use "talking" to woman... they did enough of that by themselves. Shouting and stamping had no effect either, in fact the opposite, and evolution developed a natural response for this behaviour, we now know as the crossing of the legs!!. Male and female spoke in two different languages, neither to fully understand the other again.

Anyway, as I was saying, man realised that he had to come up with something, not just anything, but some "THING" that would "pull" the birds rather than shooting them down.

- Something that would give him one up on the competition.

- Something that was removed from the lottery of birth.

- Something that was unaffected by excesses of alcohol and climatic conditions.

- Something that would be the biggest and best without the need for plastic surgery.

- Something to make him stand out in a crowd without having to drop his trousers

- Something that would keep his inadequacies unseen and his manhood intact.

  He needed some THING

- An optional extra...A complementary addition...that would gain him respect and admiration from his peers...

- Envy from lesser mortals,

- And have an effect on women that could only be described as positive!!

Hence:

THE STATUS SYMBOL

was born...and it worked

He'd finally figured it all out!!

18

19

And what about today? Well, man made himself a mechanical animal!!

No more four legged mammalian beasts, but a creation of their own doing, produced to their own specifications.

A creature that they would still have to feed and look after, but one that was so flexible in character that one need only excel in part of its life, to achieve status, respect and admiration.

THERE HAS NEVER BEEN SUCH A

DESIRABLE POSSESSION THAT

HAS BEEN THE FULFILMENT OF

SO MANY DREAMS!!

THE OBJECT?... THE CAR

THE DREAM?... TO MAKE IT COME TRUE

# THE OBJECT : THE CAR

# THE DREAM: TO MAKE IT COME TRUE !!

It was as various cars were becoming a mechanical reality for many men, that additional discoveries were made.

- Okay getting from A to B was no big deal, but the style in which you did it, ended up counting for far more on the male status symbol score board, than ever before.

- You could forever display your tail feathers and beat the next best cock in the mating game when ever you drove up and down the road.

- You could flex your muscles of mechanical masculinity without having spent one day in the gym, in fact your car gave you body perfection, an Adonis body !!.

The car eradicated so many imperfections and inadequacies that man began to feel a great sense of security.

This creature was giving him his excellence and a perfect replacement for his dangly bits. In fact this creature began to develop a sex. Not male as one may have thought, but female!! (What a compliment girls?!)

In fact if anything came along to spoil his day,

- "She" was always there to make him feel good again.
- "She" would let him tinkle with her engine…any time.
- "She" would hum and purr and respond to his every move on the accelerator pedal.
- "She" made him feel 100% solid man!!

The result of this was that she became loved and cared for, looked after and treasured, taken out in the evening and at weekends. Wined and dined on expensive resin polish and high performance oil. A little house was provided for her and all sorts of accessories were bought as little presents to complement her paintwork and interior finish.

# ODE TO THE OTHER WOMAN

She was sleek - she was mean
she was terribly clean
she was big - she was fast
she was loyal.....
She was fun and exciting
and very inviting
and he was all covered
in oiL!!

Her metal fatigued him
her leather so pleased him
but one day he took it
too far.....
... He dumped the ol' woman
cos he knew he could pull 'em
and left home to live
with the car!!

So when you hear natter
and a bit of a clatter
With an engine that gurgles
and roars.....
Remember the story
of mans "shining glory"
And how it out shone
all of yours!!

So all over the world today there are men who love their cars!!

All over the world there are women who love their men who love their cars!!

Today millions of men will have their heads stuck under a bonnet of a car, hoping to improve their chances of either winning a prize or winning a woman. Heads will be turned by the sound of exhaust and mister family man will uphold his respectability for another year thanks to his credit rating.

This book is for the women who have known and loved men like you, and for the men who have known and loved women like us....hence.....the essential guide to the ultimate act of love....

THE CAR MASUTRA !!

# THE MECHANICS OF MAN AND HIS MACHINERY

AUNTIE MARY'S UNIVERSITY THESIS PAPER ON:

THE "WHO, WHERE, HOW AND WHAT FOR"

OF HELPFUL HOUSEHOLD TIPS AND HINTS

ON THE MAN WHO LOVES HIS CAR!!

(An in depth Study!!)

Talk about a non starter, but I'm afraid that's just how it is!!

From merely looking at the presentation of the male form, there are no exterior tell tale signs that will give you any sort of a clue as to his love of cars!!

It is only through constant observation and diligent monitoring that one will become aware of the true nature of his love!!

Unfortunately, to get into such close proximity as to be able to fulfil the above, often requires some sort of relationship!!

- If you gave birth to him and he calls you "Mother" ... It's just been part of the job!!

- If he's a real little pain ... you probably call him brother and have to put up with him!!

- And those who fall in love with him? ... TROUBLE!!

# THE MAN... THE DATE...
## THE CAR

Unknown to us at this stage is that this man has anything else on his mind except us!! We are totally unaware of the time, effort and hole in his bank balance that this mode of transport has cost him, but.... to be fair, it really is rather nice him having this fab car that he's just waiting for <u>us</u> to get into!!!

So what can we do to protect ourselves from his offers and proposals? His sweet talk and generosity? His aftershave and charming manner? His ultimate pull machine?... HIS CAR!!

Well — you can either refuse a ride and close the door, or you can enter into his world with a little knowing look on your face!! (Don't make it too obvious, there'll be time to check the size of his tool kit later!!)

THE FIRST DATE !!

So during this first outing, what are the indications that should raise our suspicions? What points of perception should we acquire regarding his car....

- The smug smile of pride on his face?
- The blinding gleam of his paintwork?
- The g-force on acceleration?
- The deep throb of the engine?
- His look of horror when we slam his door shut?
- The lack of mud on the wheel arches?
- A full description of how the car will look?
- The producing of a car photo album?

Well girls .... It's the lot!!

But now is the time to enjoy every moment with him. The wild and fun activities with the care free spirit of love in the air.... but beware "The point of no return" You'd be surprised at how fast a woman's mind can work, in the right conditions boys!!

By now, you WILL have passed "the point of no return!!"

Yes.... you read and noted the list of suspicions on the previous page, you were fully aware of getting into his car, that he was already scoring high marks on "points of perception", but you have wantonly and abandonly left all sense of reason and adult responsibilities behind you, and fallen in love!!

Unfortunately, this heart condition gives you extremely bad eyesight, and can often lead to total blindness because you love HIM!! You see.... the hours of labour or financial investment HAVE paid off... he's done it...it worked!! NOW he can get back to being himself again, with the knowledge that his car has performed well beyond the call of duty!!

Your days of total attention are now numbered — the questions repeat themselves — your mind is churning.... the awesome conclusiion is reached...

# HE'S A CAR LOVER !!!

BE YOU - GIRLFRIEND, WIFE, MOTHER OR SISTER

HIS HEART IS TAKEN!... HIS LOVE IS ACCOUNTED FOR!

# THE MAN WHO LOVES HIS... CAR

Here's a little ditty written just for you

It's a girlie opinion to a "boys own view

Talk of mechanics and the manly pretension?

Admit that your car is a willy extension!

All of the time and the money and devotion

Put those pretty little racing wheels in motion

You put her to bed – you keep her dry – the reason why?

Make the girls go Ohh

Makes the guys go Ahh

He's the man who loves his...car!!!

Siliconed her engine and you rubbed her paint

Lubricated joints until very late

A little bit of rust, but you got the filler

Racing oil, and the finish is a killer

Deep throbbing sounds as you turn her over

Straight through exhaust so you know what to give her

Walnut dash – seats of hide – come on give us a ride!?!

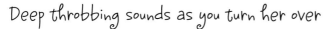

And the girls go Ohh
And the guys go Ahh
He's the man who loves his... car!!!

Top gear, throttle, and then the clutch went hard
So he fiddled with the tube and the fluid shot a yard
He made an alteration to his fuel injection
Changed the starter motor — got another suspension
Careful how you drive her — Cos your big end will go
Your fuel pump is sticky and your gaskets will blow!
So let me fix your engine — leave it all to me —
Need an M.O.T?!!!

(nudge, nudge — wink, wink)

# WHAT TO DO NOW

Well done for getting this far

Now is the time to have a little think....

A pause in the proceedings....

A day on your own to take stock of what life has sent your way

## ALTERNATIVES

1. Issue divorce proceedings naming the car as the third party on grounds of adultery
2. Demand he makes a choice between you or his car
3. Try and win him back
4. Try and understand him
5. Try and impress him
6. Try and accept him

Lets look into it together.....

# DIVORCE

Issue divorce proceedings may seem a good idea at the time, but it is also likely to bring your lawyer out in a fit of hysterical laughter!! You may feel you are within your legal rights by naming the car as the third party on grounds of adultery, so...

If you need cheering up.... have a go!!

# DEMANDING ANSWERS

## "Me or the Car"

Look at him in the cold light of day

Not a pretty sight.....

Late meals, extra laundry, oil spills on the drive, engine bits in the kitchen.

And where do you fit in all of this?

An extra pair of hands?

Yes.... you have it!!

A good old 'huff and puff' and some bitter complaining will only confirm that he has made the right decision buying the car?!

If you don't like it, he's expecting you to pack you bags and leave him in peace.

He wants a partner, not a pain!!

# WIN HIM BACK

You've got a lovely cylinder

You've got a good suspension

You've got some lovely gaskets

And a lovely fuel injection

You've got a lovely engine

And you passed the M.O.T

So leave the car outside for once and come inside with me?

I'm waiting...... I'm waiting

.... I'm waiting

Win him back? .... You won't!!

# UNDERSTAND HIM

## "...You Might"

This is regarded as one of the ultimate feats of patience and endurance that a woman may ever undertake!!

This act of love being so great that it has even led to manual assistance and getting out the resin polish ready to give the car a rub down!! If you love him... It's worth a chance!!

Men.... Please appreciate the effort!!

UNDERSTAND HIM !!

# IMPRESS HIM

Actions speak louder than words, but here are a few tips to ensure you keep his attention regardless of his first love... the car.

1. Learn what the little numbers on the back of your car really mean "1.3" what and how?

2. Buy him the bits he keeps on going on about at Christmas and Birthday presents.... always think cars.... he does!!

3. Get very excited when he is.... even if your not quite sure what all the fuss is about Just keep smiling a lot and saying "Oh Yes!!"

4. Tell other people not to touch his paintwork.

5. Go "Woooo!!" Every time he puts his foot flat out on the accelerator.

6. Never take too much luggage other wise he'll have to make the awkward decision of whether to take his toolbox out of the boot or not!!

7. Get very silly and cute.... run up and give his car a kiss and tell her how pretty she is.

8. Complain to him about dried-on mud on other people's wheel arches.

9. Tell him that even if he didn't have his car.... he would still be wonderful.... blah, blah, blah.

10. Start looking after your own car and keeping it clean and shiny.... the message must start to sink in soon.

11. Remember the quirks of his car.

12. Read up on differential unit ratios and then give your point of view in the pub.

13. Tell him he can use your car, when it's raining.

14. Never look or act embarrassed when the car breaks down in front of a million and one fellow motorists... a hard one.

15. Possess a very large photo of his car....only.

16. Body paint yourself in the same colour as the car.

17. Replace your overnight face cream with wax polish and filler.

18. Construct a car outfit to wear during the cold winter nights together!! It'll beat the socks off stockings and suspenders, cos he won't be able to resist getting his hands on the engine!!

You may not be his first girl,

But he'll certainly know you're different!!

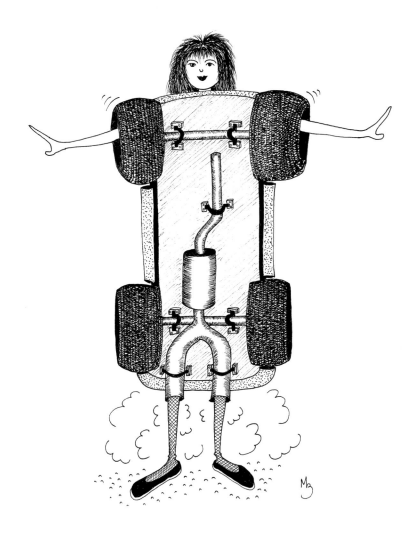

IMPRESS HIM !!

53

# ACCEPT HIM

O.K you've won.... you've got me

There's no more I can do

But lie back and accept the fact,

There's no one quite like you!!

It's hard to understand it, why

.... I love you as you are?

So I will be the woman

To the man who loves his car.


(Puke....sick....get a bucket quick!!)

ACCEPT HIM

# THE MAN WHO LOVES HIS CAR

Okay....So we're sticking with it then?
Right, Lets get down to the nitty gritty and see exactly what we've let ourselves get into here!!

Over the following weeks/months/years a vast network of Automotive Activities are going to be thrust before you, a world that up until now you would have been totally oblivious of, or simply passed by without a second glance!!

This love of his, will display itself in all sorts of shapes and sizes, degrees and measures, forms and formulations, and its all for us to understand, and really not to get too worried about it all!!

I'LL throw you in at the deep end... "making love!!"

## THE MISSIONARY POSITION (FIG 1)

The most commonly used and widely practiced form of making love!! It is totally acceptable, but if he can't get it right... there's little chance that he will get up to anything else!!

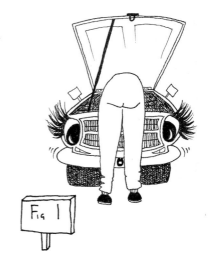

Fig 1

## THE READERS DIGEST REPAIR MANUAL POSITION (FIG 2)

Is really regarded as extended fore-play, rather than anything else. It is a bit of a tinkle, some fumbled fiddling and then back indoors for a cup of tea!!

Fig 2

BASIC LOVE MAKING POSITIONS!!

## THE CAR MANUAL POSITION (FIG 3)

Is really the first position that should get you thinking!! He's beginning to get a bit serious now!!

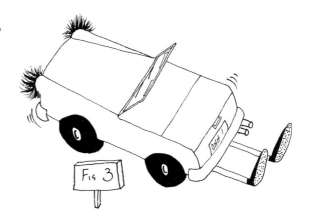

## THE "LETS SEE WHAT'S AT THE OTHER END" POSITION (FIG 4)

This is the point at which you Loose him!! You'll normally catch him at it over a weekend, although a large group of men are actually paid to do this on a 9 to 5 basis....the Garage Mechanic!!

BASIC LOVE MAKING POSITIONS !!

Fig 5

Fig 6

Fig 7

POSITIONS FOR THE MORE ADVANCED!!

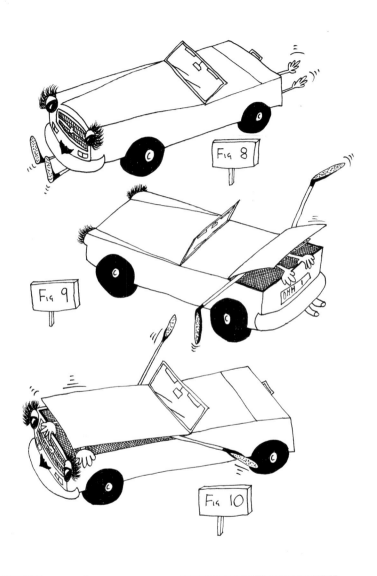

Fig 8

Fig 9

Fig 10

POSITIONS TO CAUSE CONCERN!!

61

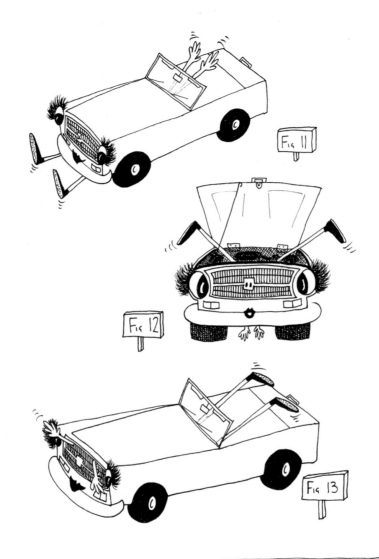

Fig 11

Fig 12

Fig 13

"A Very Advanced Medical Condition"
Positions!!

There are, which is of great concern to me, a poor group of unfortunate young men with no car to their name. These "mechanical stallions" are starved of satisfaction and fulfilment, and will spend many a restless night tossing... and turning, trying to work out the best approach to take, plucking up the courage to ask that vital question: "Can I borrow the keys to your car Mum?"...please?" An alternative can be used by replacing the word "Mum" with "Dad" but the outcome is not normally as successful as the first, since men want to encourage their sons own route to self discovery!!

Fig 14

THE MANUAL WORKERS POSITION

One should be in a strong position now to be able to tell at a glance, exactly what the man who loves his car is up to!!

Yes.... I know it can come as a bit of a shock, but it may help a little, if you look at him more on the lines of:

"A MECHANICAL GYNAECOLOGIST"

The two professions being very closely linked, the only difference being the components of the subject matter!!

So, whatever his story line....
at least YOU now know just what he's up to!!

# A GUIDE TO HIS PILLOW TALK

Before I Continue, just a quick run through of a few "words" that he may use at the end of a "hard day". Please....don't Let them cause you concern, unless you end up having to run him to the Casualty Unit one day with car in tow!!

- Engine Mountings: He's probably tried it.

- Gear Box Mountings: He's probably thought about it.

- Diff Mounting Kit: He's probably preparing for it.

- Solid Rack Mount Kit: NOT for the faint hearted.

- Rod End's: It may well NOT just be a spanner in his pocket.

- Door Skin: ALL "fore" doors have them, except circumcised model

- Hood Bag: One size fits all.

- Bulk Head Side Panels: For a perfect stand every time.

- Brake Shoes: He MAY well attach them to his feet.

- Couplings: Two cars, two best mates...say no more?!

# GETTING TO GRIPS WITH ADDITIONAL ACTIVITIES

### "THE GIRLIES GUIDE"

# BUYING A NEW CAR

*"The Blind Date"*

Nothing gets the heartbeat racing more than reading an advert, or hearing about a car for sale within ones price range!

An early morning start is no problem....

Food is secondary

Appointments are cancelled...

Christmas can be put on the back burner for a day or two

The sheer excitement of "Could this be the one?" is all that is on his mind.

"What will she look like?!"

"Will she fancy me?!"

"Will she need any work doing to her?!"

This is not the day to expect anything, other than one very excitable man!! ...Let him go!!

# STRIPPING

## "The Strip-Tease"

Yes girls...you know what men are like.

Anything that can be, will be stripped.

Engines, gear boxes, paint work, diff units, brakes, etc.

Money will be parted with to go to re-build seminars.

If the news gets around of anybody taking something off or out of their car, he will be subjected to an irresistible urge to be there.

Mates may also pop around and ogle at engine bits for hours, often placed in sterile conditions of the kitchen!!

Nothing beats the excitement of a body shell slowly being removed to reveal all the naughty bits!!

Oh well...boys will be boys!!

THE STRIP - TEASE !!

71

# THE CAR AUCTION

## "The Red Light District"

A bit of "a boys night", with everything on offer, and the highest bidder gets her!!

Will he won't he?

Should he...why not?

What will his woman say back home?

Utter temptation!!

Can he resist it?

How can he bear the tension any longer with it just sitting there for him!!

Ohhh....Yes, Yes, Yes... No... Ummm... Yes!!

Going – Going – Gone!!

She looks great but can she perform?

By the time the night is up, you'll know just what your money has bought you!!

# MOTOR RACING

"Club Erotica"

Wow!! . . . .

The smell of the rubber, the gleaming paint jobs, the fabo-
throbo engines, the speed, the action, the sponsors tents and
that irritating little sound of a bumble bee in a jam jar every
time a car passes!!

A dreadfully expensive habit to get into....
To look and not to touch...
To wish and to dream...

And then to rev up your engine upon leaving the circuit and get
nicked by the police a mile down the road for impersonating a
racing driver!!

And all brought to you, by those products your parents used to
"ground" you for, and teachers used to put you in detention for
participating in.

Now this is what I call fun!!

75

# RALLY DRIVING

For this, the appearance of the car is not of great importance....but having a death wish is.

You need a good work horse with a powerful, reliable engine.... but NO brakes!!

A sense of adventure...to "pass over" to the other side, yet determination....to stay alive for the wife and kids.

You've got to give it all you've got...and have the insurance company clinging to their seats.

In next to no time go from start to finish...and be first!!

(This is where the little problem you've been going to see the doctor about, for the last few years can really come in handy!!)

PREMATURE ACCELERATION !!

77

# DRAG RACING

"A bit of AC DC!!"

Classified as a family day out, there are those who would be slightly sceptical as to his attitude!!

Basically the track has two almighty phallic symbols lined up side by side powered by massive thunder thigh engines that are taken apart after every 5 second burn up – and rebuilt....again...and again...and again by big muscley men!!

Everything is focused on the cars climatic performance in those few seconds!!

A bit like what the girlies get to nattering about over a coffee in the lunch hour, when recalling last Saturday night out with you!!

DRAG RACING !!

# CONCOURS

Perfection Perfected!!

These darling little examples of production line perfection and originality, may never know the joys of driving down a country lane, the wind whistling past their wing mirrors and the gentle showers of Summer refreshing their steamed up little engines....

These cars win prizes!!

Locked away by men who would make brilliant housewives, these little beauties are not available for relations to have a quick spin in after Sunday Lunch, or to make the rounds picking up the local rugby team for a pub crawl!!

No, No, No.... You won't catch this man with his trousers down!!

DINNERS READY.

VENUS

WHEELUS

SPANNUS

1ST

OBJECT D'ART

[PUBLIC WARNING]

NO DOGS, CATS, BIRDS, MOTORCYCLES
WOMEN, RELATIONS OR CHILDREN BEYOND
THIS POINT OF PERFECTED HISTORICAL
HERITAGE . . . . ALSO . . . . . .
NO ICE CREAM, CHOCALATE, CRISPS OR
FOOD WITH DROPY BITS . . . SO . . . .

PLEASE REFRAIN FROM BREATHING IN THIS
AREA SO AS NOT TO DAMAGE MY PAINT
JOB.                    "CONCOURS WINNER"

FINE
TOOTH
COMB
FLUID

TOOTH
PICKS

HOUSE WIFE OUTFIT

DRESSING UP BOX

PIPE
CLEANERS

COTTON
BUDS

BLACK
SHOE POLISH

SUPER SUCTION MEGA BLAST
DIRT AND DUST "GET-A-RID-
OF-IT" VACUUM OOOVER.
"TO MAKE THE GIRLS GO OOOH!"

OFF
ON

AUTO PERFECTUS!!

# CAR CLUBS

## "Getting Therapy"

"Code Named: We're only here for the beer!!"

Throughout the Country little groups of men meet up to spend an evening talking and breathing cars. Regardless of status or occupation, on these special days they are only recognised by the car they own.

This type of therapy is vitally important....it enables problems to be shared, experiences to be talked through with full support from The Fellowship of Club Members.

Some may suffer from addictions to various model numbers, others buckling under the weight of frustration due to rebuilds, or simply just being unable to get the right bit....
whatever the problem, help is at hand in the form of support, reassurance, and encouragement, a friendly barmaid and a good beer!!

# CALLING THE AA

"The Breakdown"

"Automobilics Anonymous!!"

A very distressing experience for all concerned.

Suffering an emotional breakdown normally occurs either before a major ego-boosting journey or actually during one.

After all the time, money and tender loving care you have given her, when you really need her, she won't start!!

You've planned your entry for weeks, and she decides she's had enough, drawing to a halt on the hard shoulder, a couple of miles down the road.

Huh..... Women!!

- Instant AA call out....
- Instant "good mate" phone call....
- Apply the 12 step programme... but that's another book!!

## THE BREAKDOWN !!

# MOTOR MEDIA

"The Recovery Service"

"Drug Habits!!"

A weekly or monthly "fix" of a car magazine or Motoring Programme is essential for the addict.

The organised publishing houses make vast fortunes from this drug habit and continue to tempt and encourage men of all ages to partake by printing magazines with fabulous cars on the front of them.

Television companies will get hearts racing by using low level camera angles and oral explanations of such an explicate nature that it's impossible to do anything other than "turn-on"!!

A missed magazine issue can result in severe withdrawal symptoms!!

Too many car television programmes can result in over excitement and exhaustion. Lack of them can mean hospitalisation.

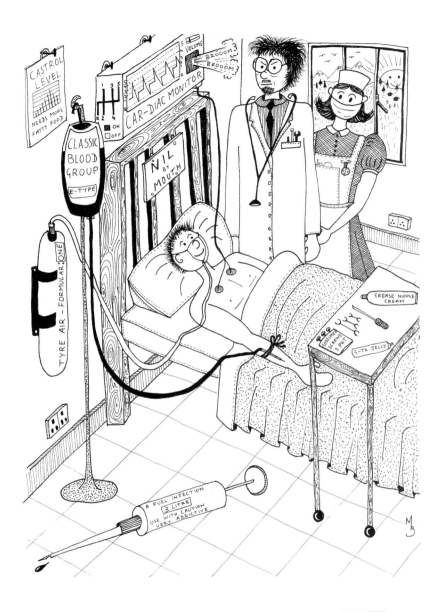

87

# CAR SHOPS

## "The Den of Iniquity"

Full of replacements and accessories, these hives of activity are numerous and well established.

Supplying everything from basic daily essentials, to love aids. Whatever his need is, the shop assistant will be only too pleased to oblige, as well as introducing him to the new products on the market.

Many an amazing story will be told to you as to the necessity of spending the money on various bits and pieces that will enhance performance or reliability!! Everyone is on the same side here, so he feels quite at home reading the small print on all the boxes.

From auto jumbles to petrol station shops, high street outlets to local dealers, temptation to buy may just prove a little too great...don't expect any change!!

THE DEN OF INIQUITY !!

# TINKERING

## "The Love-In"

Group fiddling is very popular and can cause immense bonding between fellow mates!!

When a car is loved by more than one man, two or three males may get together and work on her at the same time.

Interruptions are not welcome since once they start, they have to finish, and more often than not, "she" will present them with a host of new and exciting little problems to solve along the way..... what fun!

Don't expect regular meal times or the shelf to be put up....these men LOVE what they are doing.

Do expect to be called upon for cups of tea brought out in silence, deposited on the tarmac with a swift withdrawal back into the house.

# HEALTH HAZARDS

I could not continue with this book without bringing to your attention some very serious ailments that may befall the man who loves his car. Unfortunately, the diseases are very easy to catch, and if not caught in the early stages, can rapidly spread to the entire gang of mates!! Dire consequences follow, which have been known to interfere with ones social.....standing!!

They are as follows:

- Fluffititis

- The Flash Git Syndrome

- Rambosis

# FLUFFITITIS

Rapid action is required to prevent the spread of this infection throughout the entire car!! If this condition should appear, swiftly remove the patient from his vehicle, and administer mouth to mouth resuscitation in a very low cut dress, stressing the point that he won't be getting THIS again unless he removes the offending fluff at once!! Another form of medication which will not involve prostrating ones' body, is to give him a good spanking with glossy car magazines reiterating the fact, that he won't be getting THIS again either, if he continues with the behaviour!!

It has been known, for people to purposely attach bits of fluff to the interior of their car to create the illusion of fluffititis, in the hope of receiving treatment!!

So beware the purchase of the items depicted opposite!!

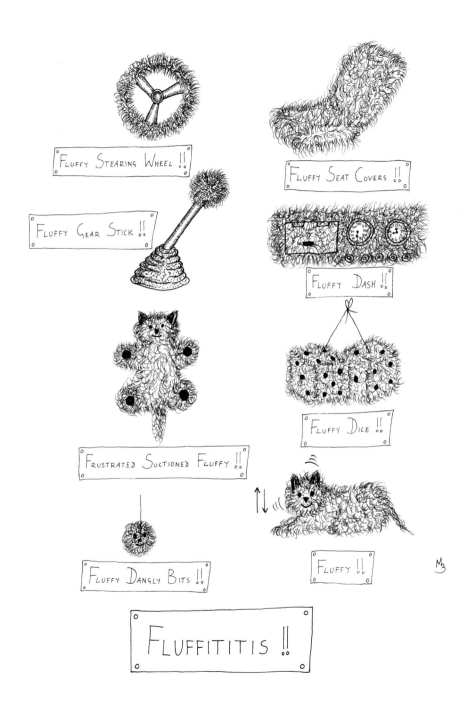

Fluffy Stearing Wheel !!

Fluffy Seat Covers !!

Fluffy Gear Stick !!

Fluffy Dash !!

Frustrated Suctioned Fluffy !!

Fluffy Dice !!

Fluffy Dangly Bits !!

Fluffy !!

Fluffitis !!

# THE FLASH GIT SYNDROME

This disease normally first appears in late teens, and can be detected by the purchase of a clapped out 2nd hand vehicle. Although it is possible to live with this addiction, the severity of the symptoms are very much down to the individual!! There are two situations which can bring this disease to its' full strength: One, is too much money..... The other is not enough!!

Trendy sunglasses are normally enough to first raise ones suspicions. Also very loud music blasting out of a wide open car window rain or shine, should also be looked upon as an indication of this disease.

In later life, this infection can lead to the purchase of classic, collectable, or very expensive cars, in order to retain ones creditability amongst peers — the cure?

They tend to grow out of it upon the birth of their first child — the baby seat blows the lot!!

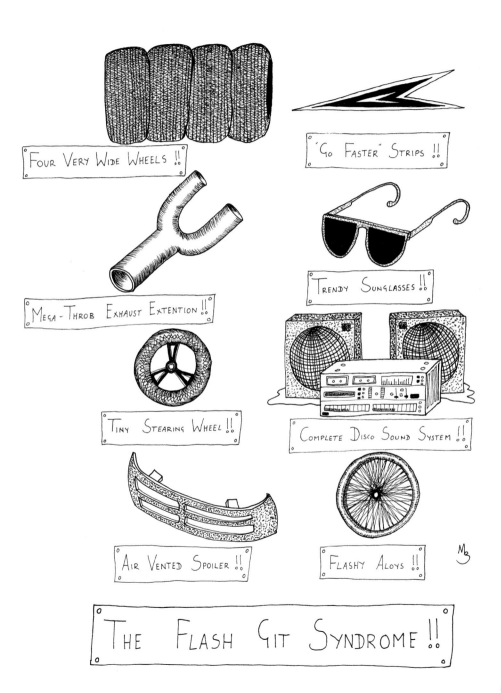

Four Very Wide Wheels !!

"Go Faster" Strips !!

Mega-Throb Exhaust Extention !!

Trendy Sunglasses !!

Tiny Stearing Wheel !!

Complete Disco Sound System !!

Air Vented Spoiler !!

Flashy Aloys !!

The Flash Git Syndrome !!

# RAMBOSIS

This is a mental disorder in which the subject believes Her Majesties Government built the entire road system specifically for themselves. Each man affected by the illness, thinks that he should be first....other motorists failing to abide by his claim to the road surface and right of way, face the possibility of being drawn to battle!!

Roundabouts, traffic lights and motorway overtaking are prime war zones, together with traffic jams, parking spaces and old people in cars, who won't pull over and let you pass!!

The calming effect of a woman's voice seems only to aggravate the matter, so just breathe deeply and remember those ante natal classes!

Remember the best remedy for Rambosis is head down, mouth shut.

RAMBOSIS

# FOR MEN ONLY

Okay guys....the tables are turned.

I know its not easy for you at the best of times....you do very well putting up with us lot, but surely a few tips and hints thrown in your direction wouldn't go amiss.

If we can learn to UNDERSTAND each other a little more, then SIMPLE misunderstandings can be AVOIDED.

It should all add up to a happier more peaceful, enjoyable life between the two sexes!!

(Don't laugh...I'm trying to do my best here!!)

# KNOW THE ENEMY

*"Foreign Bodies"*

Before the purchase of any metal, there may appear a species of human existence whose sole intent is to prevent monies being parted with for the fulfilment of your dream!!

These beings come in all shapes and sizes, they tend to wear dresses, have heels on their shoes, and let you jump into bed with them on a fairly regular basis.

Unfortunately, they spend most of their time appearing to be speaking a totally different language to yourself, which can make them very difficult to understand at the best of times.... and there may be little chance you ever will.... Accept it....

females!!

THE WIFE !!

THE GIRLFRIEND AND GIRLFRIENDS BEST FRIEND !!

THE MUMMY !!

THE SISTER !!

THE AUNTIE AND NEXTDOOR NEIGHBOUR !!

THE GRANNY !!

FOREIGN BODIES !!

# FINDING A HOME

## "The Last of the Tool Shed"

Another area of contention may be housing...not only for the car you are about to restore, but the host of extras that you purchase for the job!!

Before you start a project it is important to look at lots of glossy books on the subject that give you NO indication of the task ahead. The last thing you want to do is be put off the idea!!

(The music from "The Sound of Music" "Doe a Deer")

Let's start at the very beginning
A very good place to start
When you read you begin with A B C
When restoring it looks so...E-Easy  E-Easy
Pictures in books showing how she will look
E-Easy E-Easy
E-Easy Peesy  Easy Peesy  Easy Peesy  Easy.

Big mistake Number One!!

THE LAST OF THE TOOL SHED!!

# FINDING A MATE

"Perfect Partners"

A very essential piece of equipment when restoring a car is a good mate.

These come in allsorts of shapes and sizes and are very often drinking buddies.

Before you commence on a project it is very important to have their support, and without a lot of effort, you'll no doubt get a good deal of encouragement from them as well.

Please remember that by them saying "Yes" to your idea does not make them legally responsible for your state of mind or bank balance as the months/years go by!!

You will be spending a lot of time together though, with greatly increased telephone communication, so when finding a perfect partner....

Choose wisely!!

THE CLIVE  THE GRAHAM  THE PETER  THE NICK

THE MARTIN  THE JONATHAN  THE RICHARD  THE ROBERT

PERFECT PARTNERS!!

109

# A PAUSE FOR THOUGHT

"The New Arrival"

You've cleared the garage.

Got rid of, or round the "enemy" by increasing the house-keeping or a couple of good meals out.

Your best mate has said "Yes" to the whole idea after a night down the pub!

Now you have her where you want "her"
....Sitting in your back yard!!

You can admire "her" rust damage, "her" broken suspension, "her" torn seats, "her" blown up engine, her flat tyres and her sad little face....she's been waiting for you!!

With tools to hand, and a committed heart, the day has finally arrived. All you have got to do now is decide WHAT to do first!!

# .... SO

The excitement and energy flow....days are short and nights are long....but how on earth can you keep this love affair with your car going for day after day, weekend after weekend, month after month and year after year? The only way to do it is to have a small insight into a woman's mind.

Don't worry...it's not too painful.

It may be the saving of your whole restoration project, or the rescue remedy for letting you zoom around in your little number!!

So...here we go!!

# READY?!!

Are you sitting comfortably?
Then I'll begin.

If you only knew how little it takes to keep a woman happy!!

Many a man has had "Gods Gift" eating out of their hands and lost it all out of sheer pride and neglect!!

Remember your woman has stood by you through thick and thin (as the Actress said to the Bishop!!) or to put it another way...a bird in the hand is worth two in the bush!!

A woman, who loves you AND your car, is an easy life...
DON'T BLOW IT.

You're a lucky man....BELIEVE IT.

# PSYCHOLOGY

We will now have a short lesson in female psychology.

How to make her feel special:

Probably the most important thing to a woman!!

- Tell her that when is all said and done, you do love her more than your car (a little white lie now and again is acceptable ....remember all she needs to HEAR are the words!!) Another version of this is promising her that she can have a go at driving your car, but never quite get around to it!!

- To prove your love, simply 'grit your teeth' and drive your precious car down a muddy country lane or in the rain...this will prove beyond a shadow of a doubt that she has nothing to worry about, that you do love her more than your car!!

- Thank her very dearly for the replacement car bit you've already got, that she buys you for your birthday!! It's not so much the gift, as the fact she had the nerve to wander into the local motor spares shop, by herself, looking like a virginal lost soul, trying to explain to the lad behind the counter exactly what it is she was after!! (And it wasn't what the Shop Assistant proposed first off either!!)

- Be gentle when she gets major car terminology wrong in public!! She's obviously been doing some homework and is only trying to do her best...the best thing to do is laugh...you can cringe with embarrassment later on!!

- Let her feel she's really helping you, even though for that afternoon everything may take a little longer!! Putting her in charge of the wheel jack with you working away under the car, may be putting a little too much faith in your charming personality, but there's certainly no harm in giving her instructions regarding your specifications for cleaning the interior!

- This is the best one of all, the one that could give you your cake, and be able to eat it!! It's a little way of getting round the question "oh no...you're not working on THAT car again?"

Basically, when you buy your wreck, say a car that has been stuck in a farm yard for 20 years, but fully restored would be a fabo motor, tell her it's her Birthday present and that you will very kindly do it up for her!!

Or if she questions the price of your new car and do you really need it, explain that you've bought it for her! I mean would you men really spend all that money on yourself?... Surely not!! Remember, it can be registered in her name, but as long as you're paying the finance you still have control...easy eh?!

Better still – just buy it for her, .....cash!!

She will think you are wonderful, and it will almost guarantee you, hassle free years of ecstacy in the garage tinkering away to your hearts content, or driving around in the car you always wanted

It didn't take much did it?!!

# CONCLUSION

The man who loves his car.....what an inspiration he is to us all.
For these are men who display the quantity and quality of their
love for all to see...how could we possibly live without them?!

We would miss seeing the examples of sheer classic elegance
driving on our roads today.

We would miss having a smile brought to our faces when Jo
Bloggs down the road decides to jack up his suspension and use up
the multi-coloured selection of paints in the garden shed to
enhance his sex appeal!!

We would miss out on hours of fun driving along the motorway
working out who was who — by the combination of little GTX and
i and L's stuck on the back of the company car!!

We would miss the anticipation, of one day perhaps asking 'that'
person why they actually stuck their "I've been to a Wild Life
Park" sticker on their car!!

We would miss the rows of glossy car mags lining the shelves at the News Agents!!

We would miss the action of the Grand Prix (actually.....are you free later on?...I could do with a bit of that!!)

We would miss Car Shows, Rallies, Fun Rides, TV Programmes.

We would miss excellence in Engineering and Design, and the heroes of this Industry and Profession.

We would miss the hours of fun, speed and excitement; in fact, we would ALL miss having a ride....or being taken for one!!

Mans ultimate status symbol, has now become a necessity...clever one boys!!

So me?... Well I'm off to bed now!!

This book has all been written with the greatest of affection for the man who loves his car and the women involved in and with men and cars.

From the 17 year olds who are on their first car, to the Business Executive, to the wide boy!!

From the pride and joy to the ultimate sexy beast of a machine!!

From the sentimental to the outrageous!!

From the heap of metal to the classic car!!

From the dream to the reality....

From the boy to the man....

To his car.....

His.........  LOVE

## Another great title from Left And Left Again

# "WHO SAYS WOMEN CAN'T DRIVE?"
### The Diverse World of Woman's Driving Skills!!

## By
## Mary Bird

Women are very good at driving!!
From driving him up the wall to driving him round the bend.
The world of female driving skills is looked at in humorous depth.
Why do women drive so well? ...natural talent!!

**Keep up to date with gifts for the man who loves his car at:**
www.carmasutra.com
www.forthemanwholoveshiscar.com

**The Author:**

Mary Bird is the daughter of an Anglican Clergyman. She studied speech therapy, and then trained at the London College of Fashion. As a theatrical costumier, Mary worked in film and television and had her own 'Rock Fashion' company for celebrated clients as a couturier. She has also appeared on 'Top Gear' and was a professional in the music industry. Mary now lives in East Anglia.